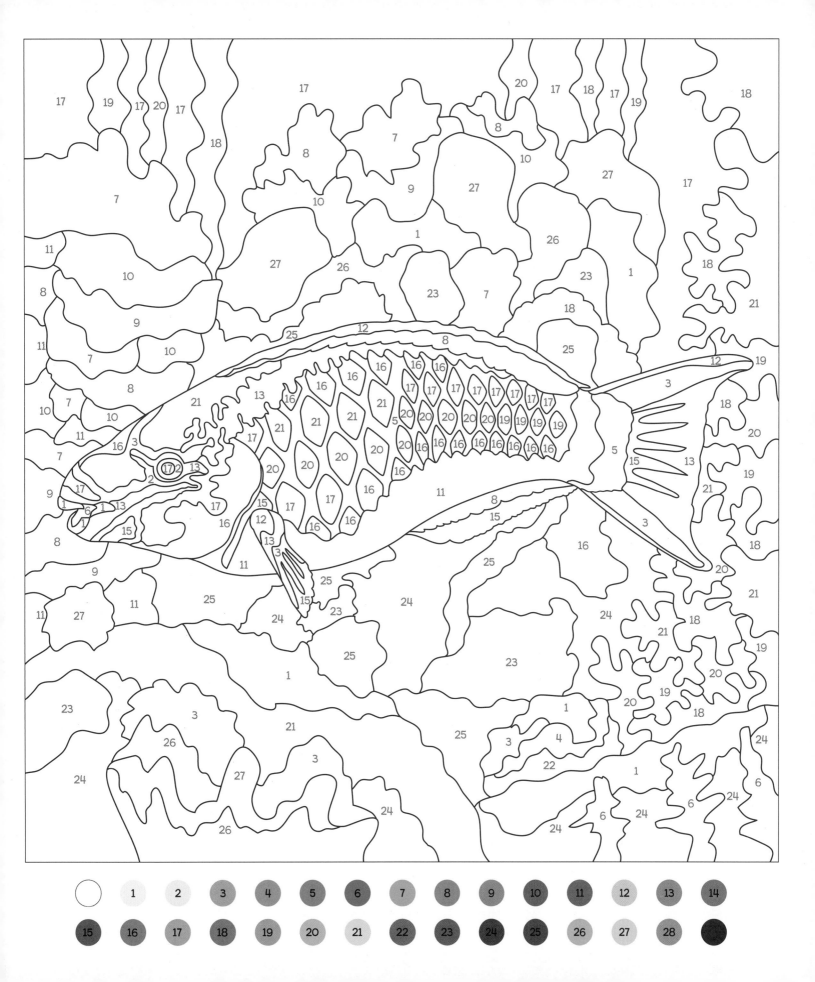

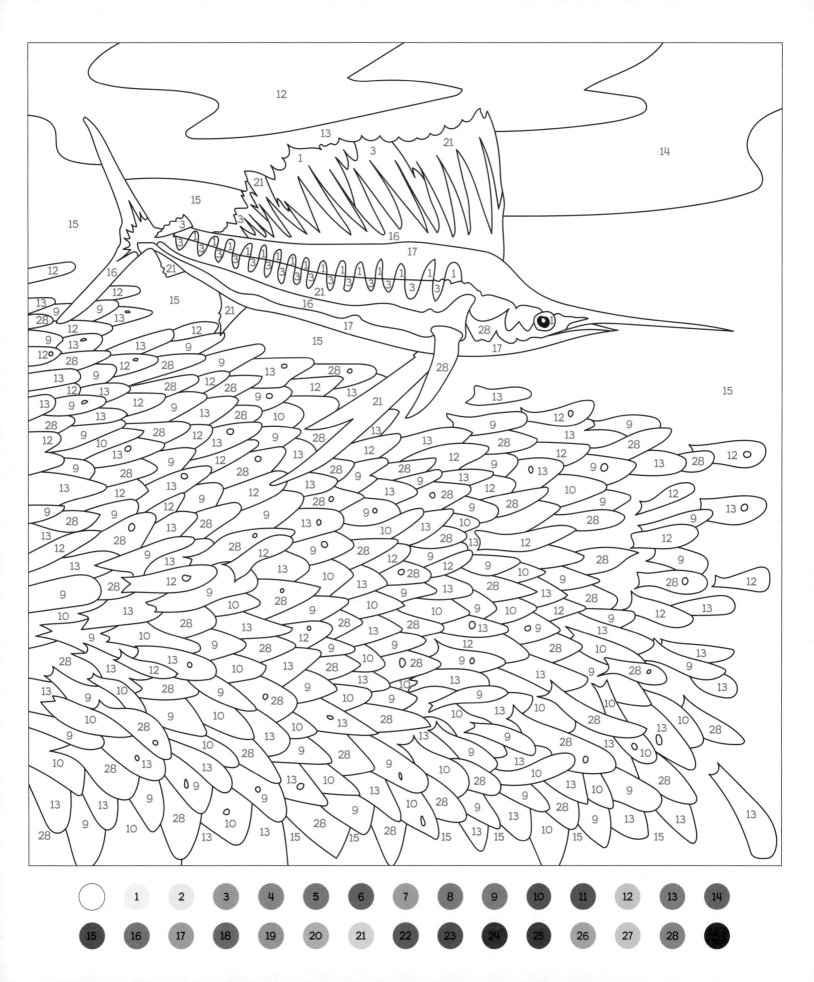

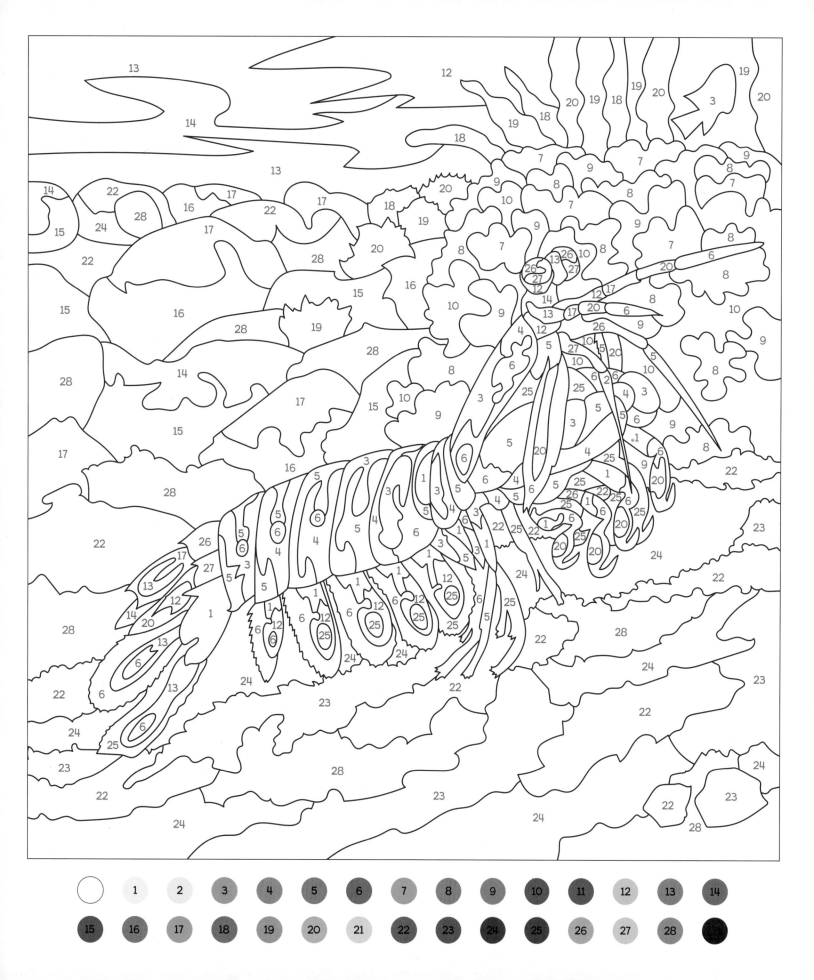

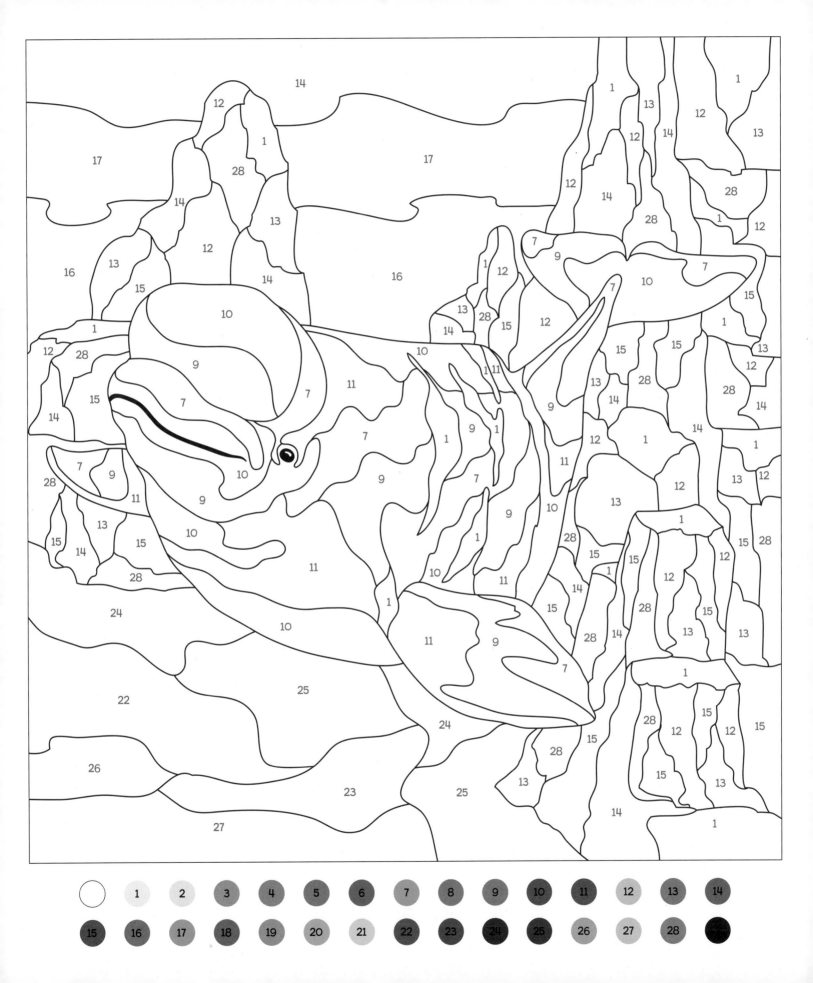

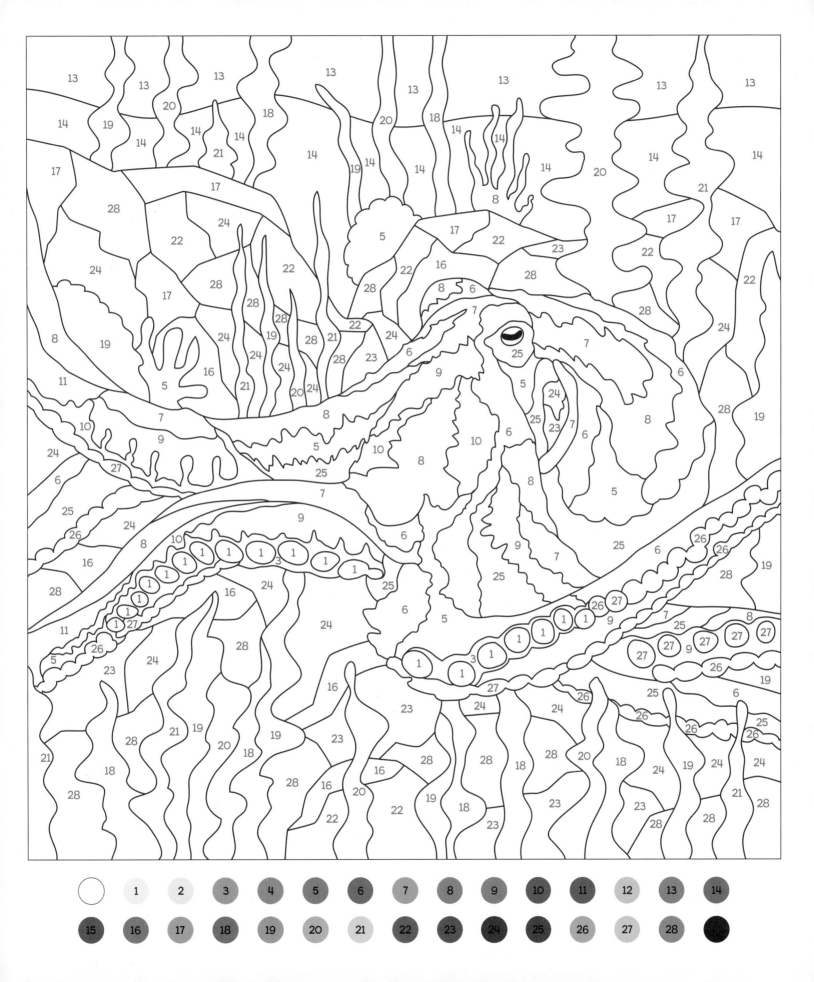

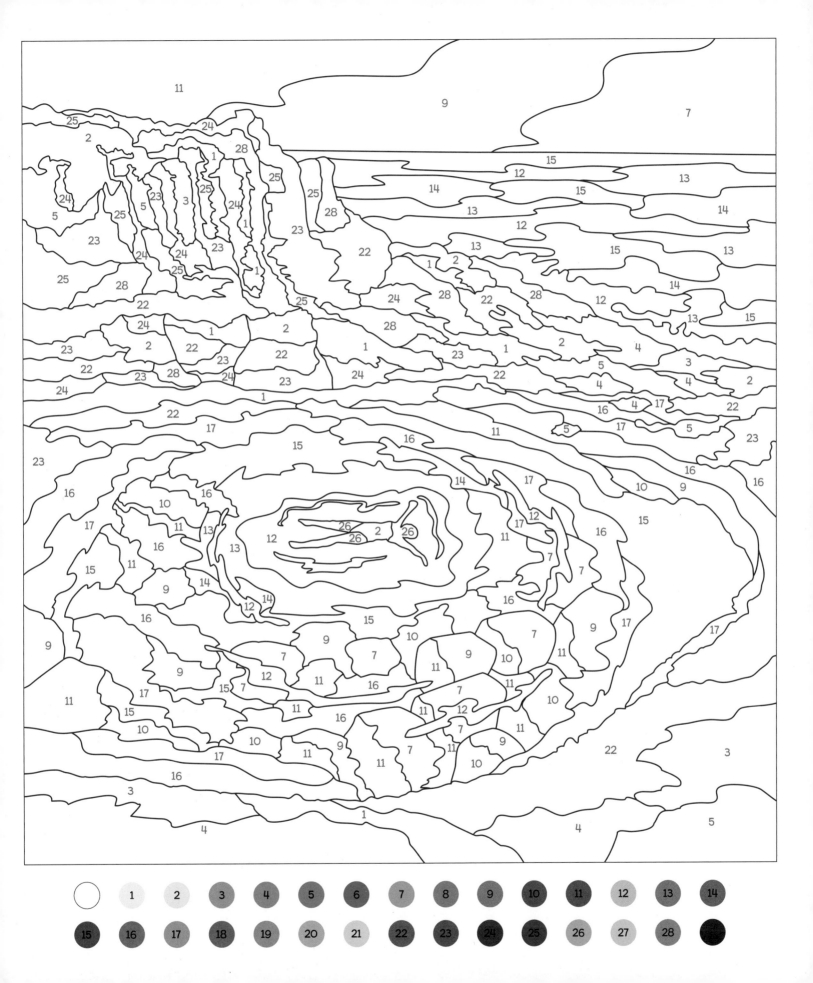

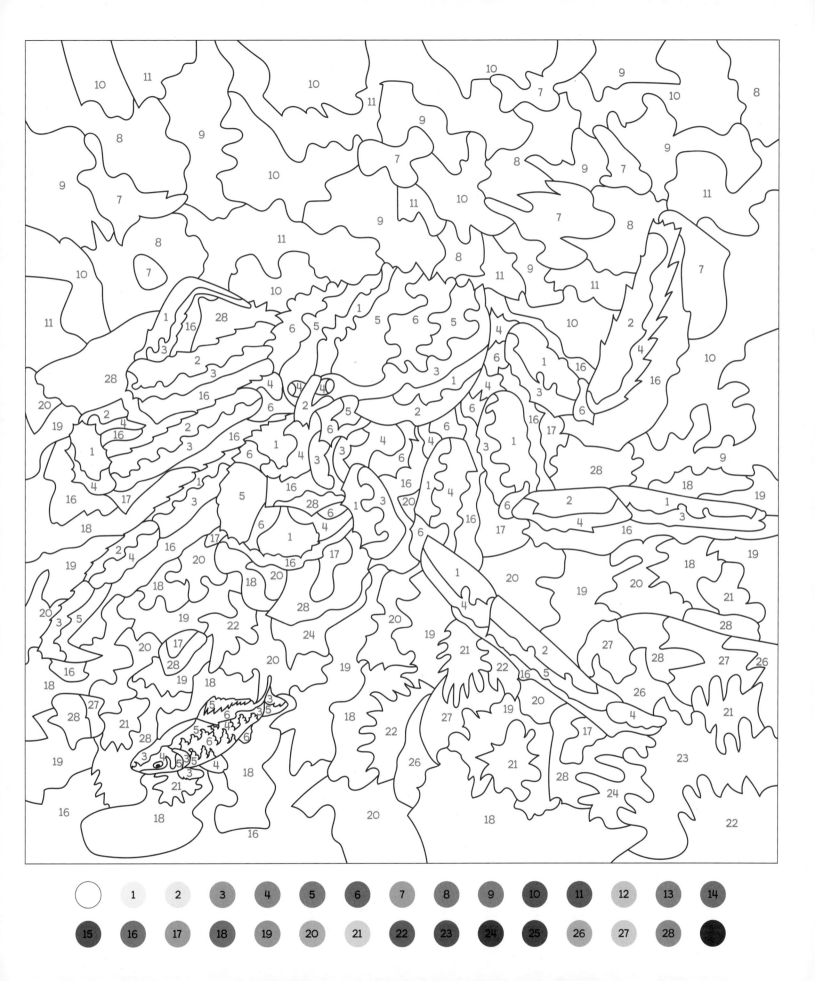

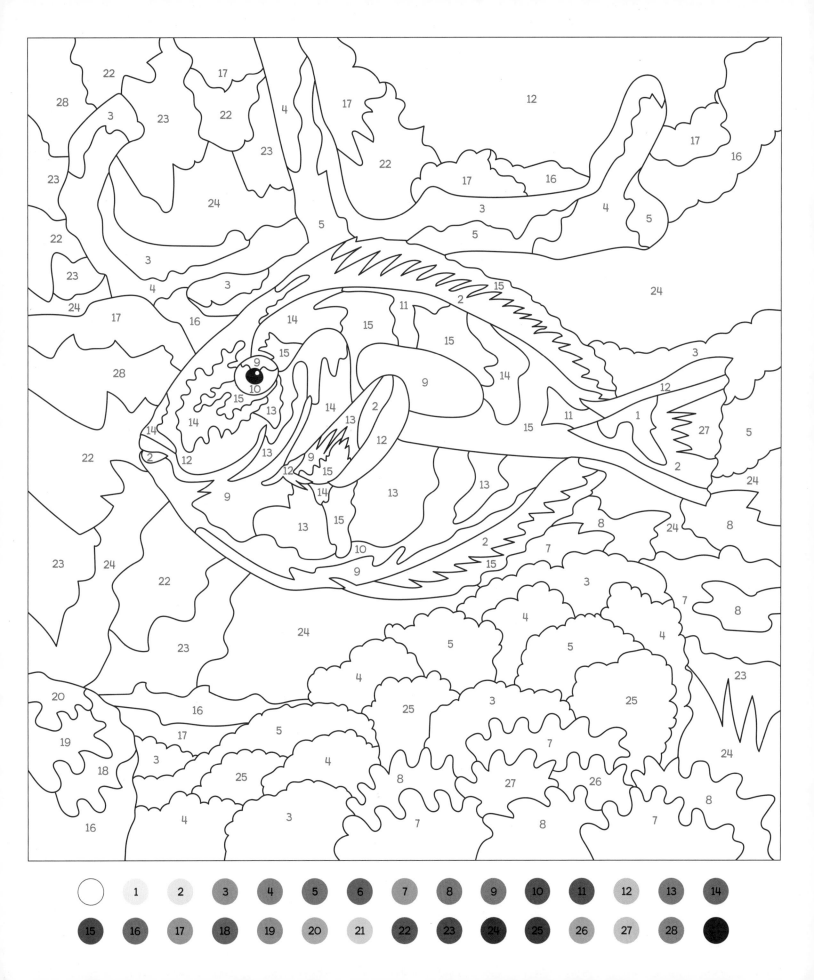

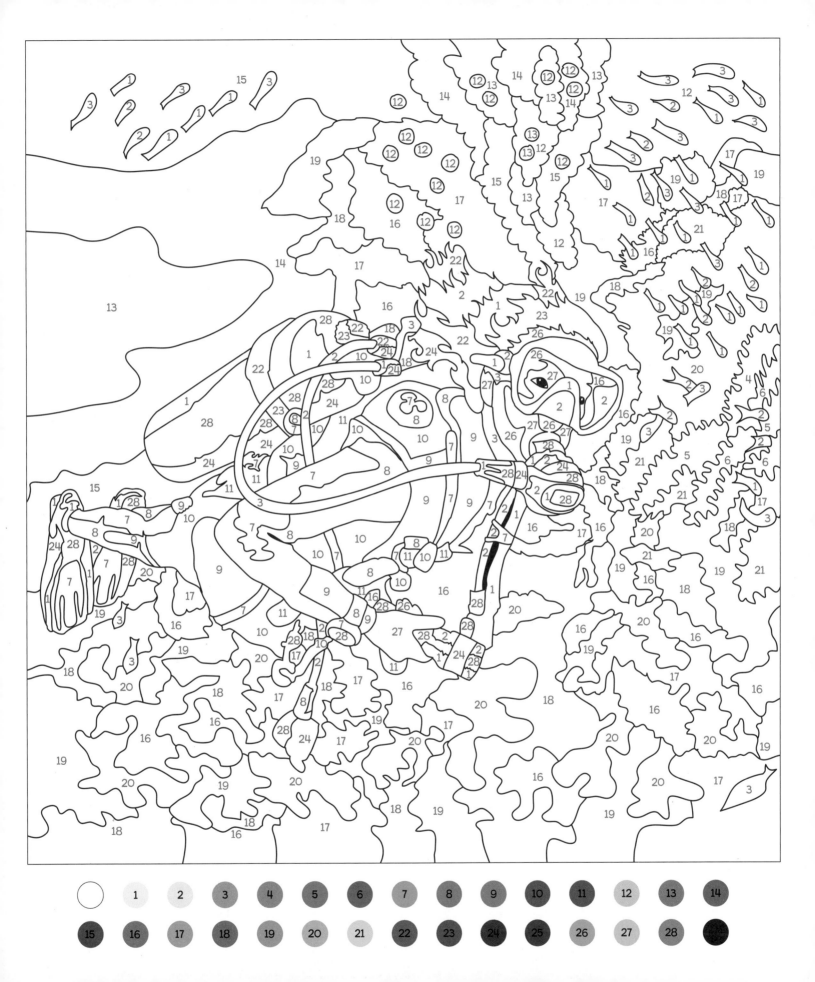

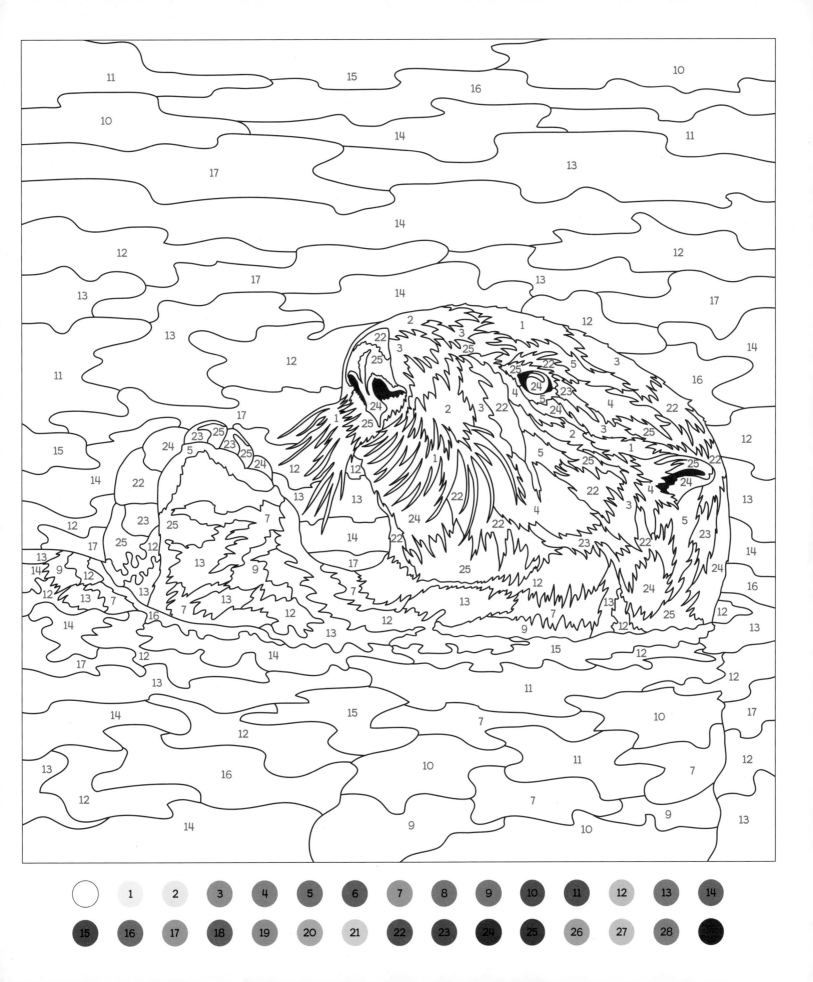

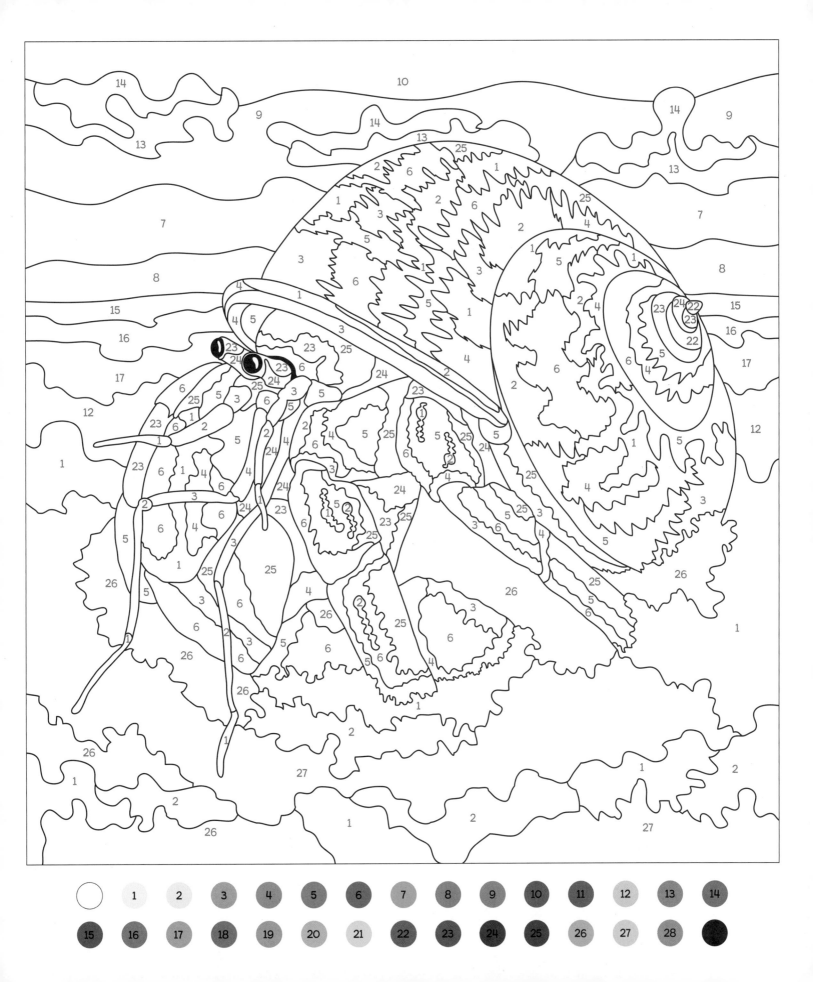

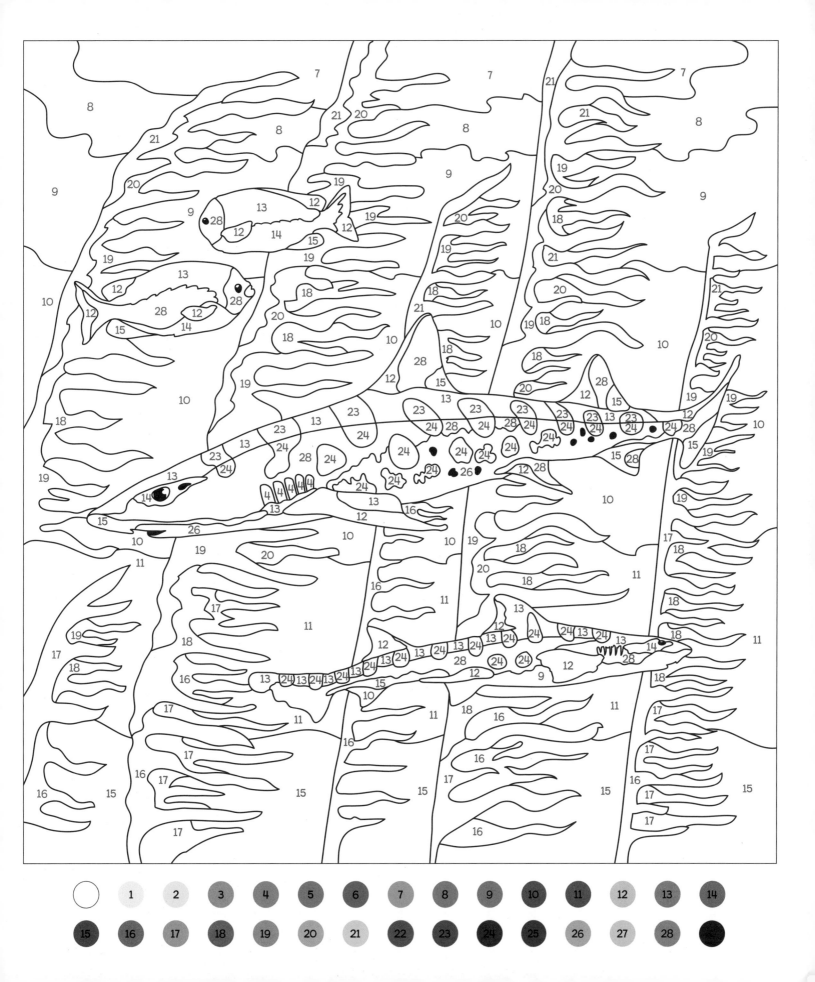

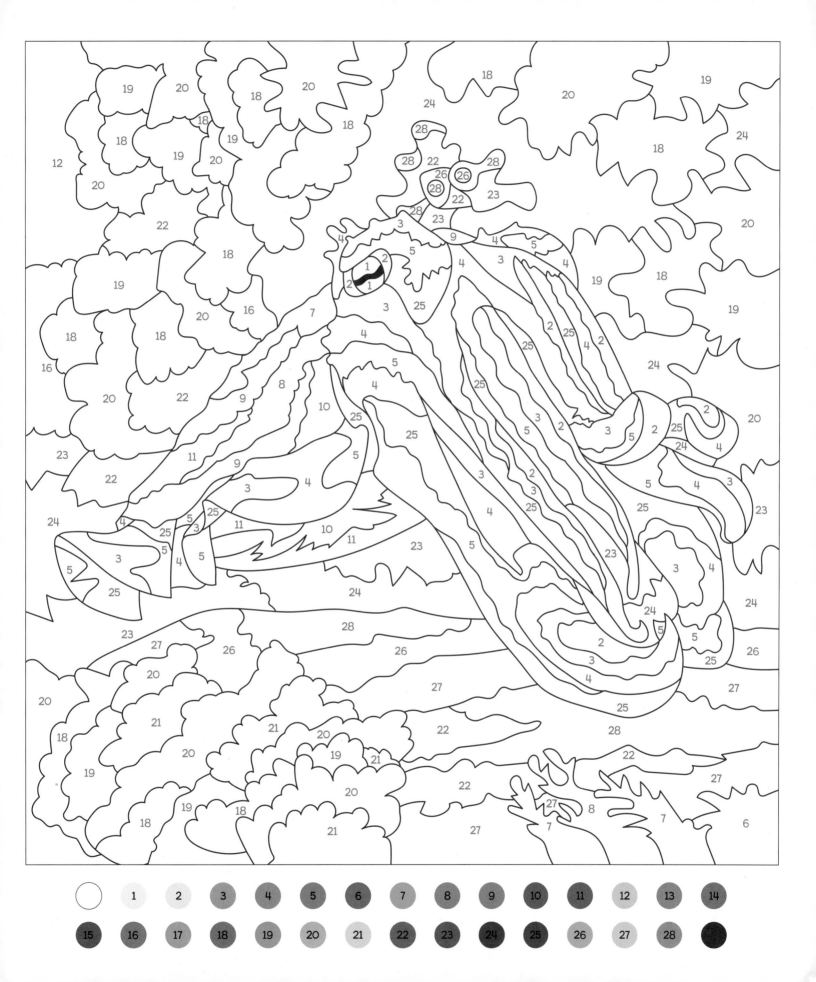

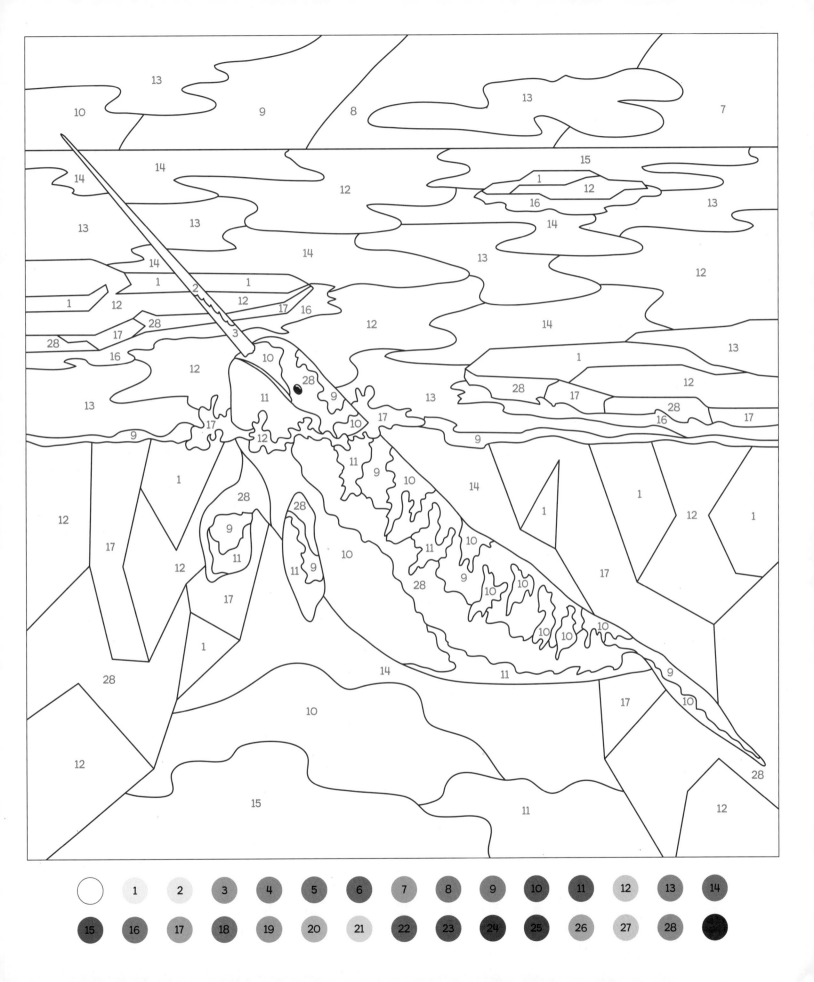

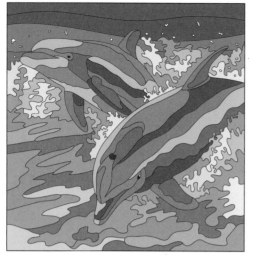

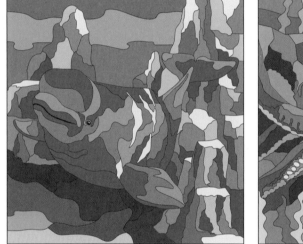
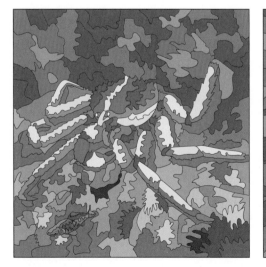

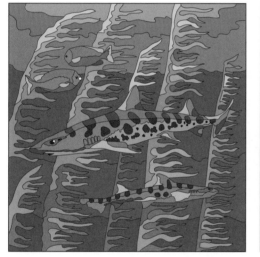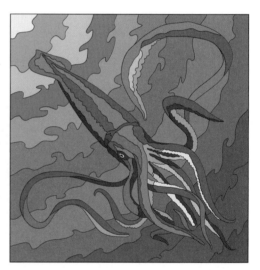

Wild Ocean
COLOR BY NUMBERS

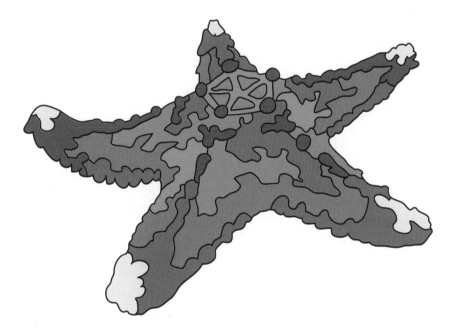

ARCTURUS

This edition published in 2022
by Arcturus Publishing Limited
26/27 Bickels Yard, 151–153 Bermondsey Street,
London SE1 3HA

Illustrations: Andres Vaisberg with Diego Vaisberg,
DGPH Design and Visual Arts Studio
Design: Tania Field
Editorial Manager: Joe Harris
Design Manager: Jessica Holliland

ISBN: 978-1-3988-1970-2
CH010339NT
Supplier 29, Date 0622, PI 00001961

Printed in China